TUNIS TRAVEL GUIDE 2026

"Discover the Best of Tunisia's Capital: From Ancient Carthage to Modern Charm"

By Leo Dakarai

TABLE OF CONTENTS

1. Introduction to Tunis
1.1 Why Visit Tunis in 2026
1.2 Quick Facts About Tunis
1.3 Best Times to Visit Tunis
1.4 What's New in Tunis for 2026

2. Essential Information
2.1 Entry Requirements: Visas and Vaccinations for Tunisia
2.2 Currency, Budgeting & Money-Saving Tips
2.3 Safety, Health & Traveler Advice
2.4 Emergency Numbers and Services in Tunis

3. Getting to Tunis
3.1 By Air: Tunis–Carthage International Airport & Flights
3.2 By Train: National and Regional Routes
3.3 By Bus or Car: Road Trips and Driving Tips
3.4 By Sea: Ferries and Mediterranean Cruise Options

4. Getting Around Tunis

4.1 Public Transport: Metro, Buses, and Shared Taxis (Louages)

4.2 Taxis, Rideshares & Car Rentals

4.3 Walking Tours & Cycling Routes in Tunis

4.4 Insider Tips for Moving Around Like a Local

5. Where to Stay in Tunis

5.1 Luxury Hotels & Resorts

5.2 Mid-Range and Budget-Friendly Options

5.3 Boutique Hotels, Guesthouses & Traditional Dar Stays

5.4 Neighborhood Guide: Medina, La Marsa, Carthage & Beyond

6. Exploring Tunis

6.1 Top Attractions: Medina of Tunis, Carthage, Bardo Museum & More

6.2 Hidden Gems: Street Art, Secret Cafés & Lesser-Known Sites

6.3 Suggested Itineraries (1-Day, 3-Day & 5-Day Plans)

7. Experiencing Local Culture

7.1 Tunisian Traditions, Etiquette & Lifestyle

7.2 Culinary Journey: Food, Drinks & Street Eats in Tunis

7.3 Festivals & Cultural Celebrations in 2026

7.4 Shopping: Souks, Handicrafts & Modern Boutiques

8. Activities & Adventures Around Tunis

8.1 Day Trips & Excursions: Sidi Bou Said, Dougga, Hammamet & More

8.2 Beaches & Water Sports Near Tunis

8.3 Nightlife: Cafés, Bars, and Live Music

8.4 Wellness: Hammams, Spas & Relaxation Spots

9. Practical Information

9.1 Language Guide: Useful Arabic & French Phrases

9.2 Connectivity: Wi-Fi, SIM Cards & Internet in Tunis

9.3 Do's and Don'ts in Tunisian Culture

9.4 Accessibility & Travel Tips for All Travelers

10. Traveler's Resources

10.1 Useful Apps, Maps & Online Tools

10.2 Embassies & Consulates in Tunis

10.3 Tourist Information Centers

10.4 Packing Lists & Trip Planning for Tunis 2026

1. Introduction to Tunis

Tunis, the vibrant capital of Tunisia, is where the ancient and modern worlds meet in a seamless dance of history, culture, and everyday life. Nestled along the Mediterranean coast, this city has been a crossroads of civilizations for over two millennia, carrying with it the legacies of Phoenicians, Romans, Arabs, Ottomans, and French colonialists. In 2026, Tunis is not just a gateway to Tunisia it is a destination in its own right, brimming with character, charm, and countless stories waiting to be discovered.

What makes Tunis so compelling for travelers is its unique balance between old-world traditions and contemporary energy. At its heart lies the UNESCO-listed Medina of Tunis, one of the most atmospheric old towns in North Africa. Lose yourself in its labyrinthine alleyways lined with vibrant souks, centuries-old mosques, and palaces that whisper tales of dynasties past. Every turn offers something new whether it's a spice merchant calling out to passing visitors, the delicate scent of jasmine drifting from a courtyard, or the intricate tilework that decorates hidden doorways.

Beyond the Medina, Tunis stretches outward into neighborhoods that showcase its modern cosmopolitan spirit. The tree-lined avenues of the Ville Nouvelle reflect French colonial elegance, with their wide boulevards and café terraces reminiscent of Paris. To the north, the chic seaside suburbs of Carthage, La Marsa, and Sidi Bou Said reveal a more leisurely pace of life, where blue-and-white houses overlook the glittering Mediterranean and lively cafés spill out onto cobbled streets.

But Tunis is not just about its aesthetics it is also a hub of Tunisian identity and culture. The city's museums, like the world-renowned Bardo National Museum, display mosaics and artifacts that bridge Tunisia's vast history, while its theaters, galleries, and music festivals highlight the country's dynamic artistic present. Tunisian cuisine adds another layer to the experience, blending Mediterranean freshness with North African spices: think couscous with seafood, savory brik pastries, or a refreshing mint tea enjoyed at sunset.

In 2026, Tunis is also looking ahead. The city is embracing new infrastructure, cultural events, and eco-conscious initiatives that make it more welcoming than ever for international visitors. Yet, despite these modern touches, what remains constant is the warmth of Tunisian hospitality a willingness to share, connect, and invite travelers into the rhythm of daily life.

Whether you come seeking history, seaside relaxation, cultural immersion, or simply the thrill of discovering somewhere new, Tunis offers all of it and more. It is a city that can be as fast-paced or as leisurely as you wish, where every traveler can carve out their own story. Tunis doesn't just invite you to explore; it invites you to experience to walk its alleys, taste its flavors, and feel its heartbeat.

1.1 Why Visit Tunis in 2026

Tunis is one of those rare cities that captures both the depth of history and the dynamism of modern life. For centuries, it has stood as a meeting point of civilizations Phoenician, Roman, Arab, Ottoman, and French and each era has left an imprint that still shapes the city's identity today. In 2026, Tunis stands out as a travel destination not only because of its heritage but also because of the way it has evolved into a lively, cosmopolitan capital that appeals to a wide variety of travelers.

For history lovers, Tunis is a living textbook. The Medina of Tunis, a UNESCO World Heritage Site, is among the best-preserved medieval cities in the Arab world, its alleyways filled with bustling souks, artisans' workshops, and grand mosques dating back centuries. Just outside the city lies Carthage, once the seat of a mighty empire, where ruins of Roman amphitheaters, villas, and baths still stand overlooking the sea. And then there is the Bardo National Museum, home to the world's largest collection of Roman mosaics, offering a glimpse into Tunisia's rich archaeological treasures.

For those seeking culture, Tunis is a hub of Tunisian identity. The city's art galleries, music festivals, and theater productions showcase a contemporary creativity that thrives alongside traditional forms of expression. Cafés in Sidi Bou Said host live music, artists' studios are open to visitors, and the streets themselves often double as stages for spontaneous cultural performances.

Travelers looking for leisure and relaxation will find Tunis equally rewarding. Its proximity to Mediterranean beaches means a day in the city can easily be combined with an afternoon of sun and sea. The seaside suburbs like La Marsa and Gammarth offer a slower pace of life, where modern beach clubs sit alongside traditional seafood restaurants. The hammams and spas, many dating back hundreds of years, also invite visitors to experience traditional Tunisian wellness practices.

Food enthusiasts will discover Tunis as a culinary adventure. The local cuisine blends the flavors of the Mediterranean with North African spices: couscous dishes prepared in countless variations, fresh seafood caught daily, hearty stews, and street foods like brik, a crispy pastry filled with egg and tuna. The café culture is equally strong, with mint tea, Turkish coffee, and local pastries forming an essential part of social life.

In 2026, Tunis is also increasingly appealing for travelers who want more than just sightseeing. The city is investing in sustainability, digital accessibility, and infrastructure to make travel smoother and more enjoyable. More direct international flights connect Tunis to global cities, new boutique hotels offer unique stays, and cultural events are being held to mark Tunisia's growing role as a bridge between Europe, Africa, and the Middle East.

Ultimately, the reason to visit Tunis in 2026 is that it offers something rare: the chance to stand at the crossroads of history and modernity, to experience a culture that is both deeply rooted and forward-looking, and to engage with a city that welcomes visitors with warmth, flavor, and vitality.

1.2 Quick Facts About Tunis

Tunis is the capital city of Tunisia and the political, economic, and cultural heart of the country. It is located on the northern coast of Africa, facing the Mediterranean Sea, and is home to over 2.7 million people in its metropolitan area. The city's location has made it a strategic point for trade and travel throughout history, connecting Africa with Europe and the Middle East.

The primary languages spoken in Tunis are Arabic and French, though English is increasingly understood, especially in the tourism sector. Tunisian Arabic, known locally as "Derja," is the dialect most commonly used in everyday conversation. French is used widely in business, education, and administration, making Tunis a bilingual city where many visitors will find communication relatively easy.

The currency used in Tunis is the Tunisian Dinar (TND), and cash is still widely preferred in local markets and small shops, though credit cards are accepted in hotels, restaurants, and larger stores. Tunis is in the Central European Time Zone (CET), which means it shares the same time as many European capitals, making it convenient for international visitors.

The climate of Tunis is Mediterranean, with hot, dry summers and mild, rainy winters. The city's weather allows for year-round travel, though different seasons offer different experiences for visitors.

In terms of connectivity, Tunis is served by Tunis–Carthage International Airport, located just a short drive from the city center. The city has a public transportation system that includes a light metro, buses, and shared taxis known as "louages." The road network connects Tunis with the rest of the country, making it an ideal base for exploring Tunisia's wider attractions.

Tunis is also home to a wide range of cultural and historical landmarks. The Medina of Tunis is a labyrinth of souks and monuments dating back to the 8th century, while the ruins of Carthage stand as a reminder of one of the greatest civilizations of the ancient world. Modern Tunis, on the other hand, is filled with contemporary cafés, galleries, and neighborhoods that reflect both European and Arab influences.

Quick facts about Tunis also include its cultural calendar. The city hosts the Carthage International Festival, one of the oldest and most prestigious arts festivals in Africa and the Arab world, as well as film festivals, music events, and religious celebrations throughout the year. Together, these facts paint a picture of a city that is as practical for travel as it is rich in character.

1.3 Best Times to Visit Tunis

Tunis, with its Mediterranean climate, offers a variety of experiences depending on the season, and the best time to visit depends largely on what travelers want from their trip.

Spring, from March to May, is one of the most recommended times to visit Tunis. The weather is warm but not overly hot, the skies are clear, and the city comes alive with festivals and outdoor activities. The jasmine blooms, gardens are green, and historical sites like Carthage are at their most inviting. This is also an ideal time for travelers who enjoy exploring the Medina and walking through Tunis's neighborhoods without the heavy heat of summer.

Summer, from June to August, is the peak tourist season, especially for those who want to combine the city with seaside escapes. The coastal areas near Tunis, including La Marsa and Gammarth, are filled with activity, and beach clubs are at their liveliest. Temperatures can be very high, often exceeding 35°C (95°F), so this season is best for travelers who enjoy sun and sea. The evenings, however, are cooler and filled with cultural events such as the Carthage International Festival, which draws performers and audiences from around the world.

Autumn, from September to November, is another excellent time to visit. The heat softens, the beaches are quieter, and the cultural season in Tunis is still vibrant. This is a perfect period for travelers who want to explore both the coast and the interior of Tunisia without the crowds of summer. Vineyards and olive groves near Tunis are also active during harvest season, offering unique experiences for culinary travelers.

Winter, from December to February, is mild compared to Europe, with temperatures rarely dropping below 10°C

(50°F). Rain is more frequent, but the city maintains a quiet charm. Winter is a great time for museum visits, cultural exploration, and a more intimate experience of Tunis without the bustle of high season. Travelers looking for deals on hotels and flights will also find winter the most budget-friendly time to visit.

Overall, the best time to visit Tunis depends on preference. For mild weather and cultural vibrancy, spring and autumn are ideal. For beach lovers and festival-goers, summer is the peak season. For budget-conscious or crowd-averse travelers, winter offers a quieter but equally rewarding experience.

1.4 What's New in Tunis for 2026

Tunis in 2026 is more exciting than ever, with new developments, events, and attractions that make it especially appealing to travelers this year.

One of the biggest highlights is the ongoing enhancement of the Medina of Tunis. Restoration projects have brought new life to historic buildings, opening up traditional houses, called "dars," as boutique hotels, cultural centers, and restaurants. Travelers in 2026 will find more opportunities to stay inside the Medina itself, experiencing the rhythms of daily life from within its ancient walls.

Transportation improvements also make travel easier in 2026. The expansion of Tunis–Carthage International Airport has increased its capacity and introduced more direct international routes, making it simpler to reach Tunis from major cities in Europe, the Middle East, and Africa. Within the city, upgrades to the metro system and the introduction of new digital ticketing options have made public transportation more efficient and tourist-friendly.

Cultural programming in 2026 is particularly rich. The Carthage International Festival is celebrating a milestone edition with expanded performances across music, theater, and dance, attracting international artists alongside Tunisian talent. The city is also hosting several art biennials and exhibitions that highlight Tunisia's growing presence in the global art scene. Street art festivals continue to transform urban spaces, turning neighborhoods into open-air galleries that reflect both tradition and contemporary creativity.

On the leisure side, new boutique hotels, eco-lodges, and high-end resorts have opened in and around Tunis, catering to different types of travelers. Culinary tourism is also thriving, with food tours, cooking classes, and new restaurants that reinterpret Tunisian cuisine for modern palates. 2026 sees a growing trend toward organic produce, slow food, and local sourcing, making the dining experience both authentic and innovative.

Tunis is also aligning itself with sustainable tourism initiatives. The city has introduced greener transport options, promoted eco-conscious accommodations, and emphasized the preservation of cultural and natural heritage. Travelers in 2026 can take part in experiences that not only enrich their journey but also contribute to the community and environment.

Finally, technology has found a place in Tunis's tourism scene. Mobile apps now provide interactive guides to the Medina, augmented reality experiences at Carthage ruins, and real-time event updates, making exploration more engaging and convenient.

For travelers in 2026, these new developments mean that Tunis is not only a city rooted in history but also a destination fully attuned to the expectations of modern visitors. It combines the timeless appeal of its heritage with the excitement of new experiences, making 2026 a particularly rewarding year to explore it.

2. Essential Information

Traveling to Tunis is an enriching experience, but like any international journey, it requires a degree of preparation and awareness. Understanding the essential information before your arrival will ensure a smoother, safer, and more enjoyable trip. Tunis is both welcoming and straightforward for most visitors, but knowing the entry requirements, handling money wisely, staying healthy and safe, and being aware of emergency contacts can make a significant difference in the quality of your stay. This chapter provides everything you need to be well-prepared before setting foot in the Tunisian capital.

2.1 Entry Requirements: Visas and Vaccinations for Tunisia

Entry requirements for Tunisia depend largely on your nationality. Citizens of many countries, including most of Europe, North America, and the Gulf states, can enter Tunisia visa-free for stays ranging from 30 to 90 days. However, it is always best to check the most up-to-date regulations before traveling, as policies can change with little notice. Travelers from countries that do require a visa should apply in advance at a Tunisian embassy or consulate, and in some cases, a supporting letter of invitation or proof of accommodation may be requested. For longer stays, work permits, or study visas, additional documentation will be necessary, and these must be arranged before departure.

All visitors must hold a passport valid for at least six months beyond their intended stay. Upon arrival, you may be asked to show proof of onward travel and sufficient funds for your time in Tunisia. Travelers arriving as part of organized tours may be subject to simplified entry procedures, though independent travelers should be prepared for standard checks. Children traveling with only one parent may need additional authorization documents, so families should verify these requirements in advance.

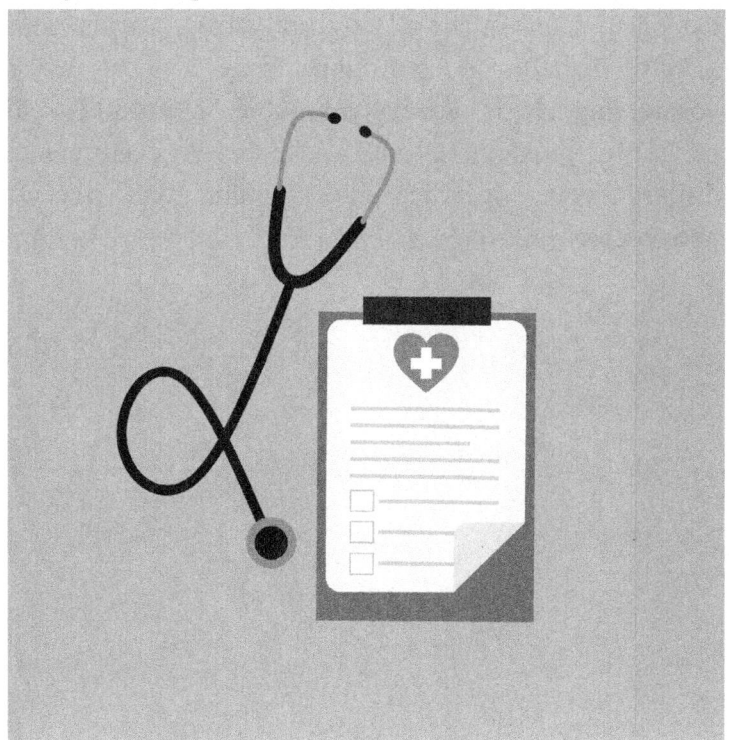

Vaccinations are not mandatory for entry into Tunisia unless you are arriving from or have transited through a country with a risk of yellow fever. In that case, proof of yellow fever vaccination may be required. While no other vaccines are compulsory, it is strongly advised that travelers are up-to-date on routine immunizations such as measles, mumps, rubella, diphtheria, tetanus, and polio. Hepatitis A and typhoid vaccinations are recommended, as both diseases can be contracted through contaminated food or water. For those planning extended stays or travel to rural areas, vaccinations against hepatitis B and rabies may also be worth considering. It is always advisable to consult your healthcare provider several weeks before departure to discuss your specific travel plans and receive personalized advice.

2.2 Currency, Budgeting and Money-Saving Tips

The official currency in Tunisia is the Tunisian dinar, abbreviated as TND. It is a closed currency, meaning it cannot be legally bought or sold outside the country. Travelers are expected to exchange their money upon arrival at Tunis-Carthage International Airport, at banks, exchange offices, or authorized hotels. Currency exchange is tightly regulated, and it is important to retain your exchange receipts if you plan to convert leftover dinars back into foreign currency before leaving Tunisia.

Credit and debit cards are increasingly accepted in Tunis, particularly in hotels, upscale restaurants, and larger shops. However, cash remains the most reliable method of payment, especially in markets, small cafés, or taxis. ATMs are widely available across the city, though travelers should be mindful of withdrawal fees and daily limits. When using ATMs, it is recommended to choose those attached to major banks for added security.

Budgeting in Tunis can be surprisingly affordable compared to many European destinations. Accommodation ranges from budget guesthouses and hostels to mid-range hotels and high-end luxury resorts. Street food and local eateries provide inexpensive and authentic dining experiences, while fine dining establishments cater to those seeking more elaborate meals. Public transportation, such as buses and the light metro, is very inexpensive, and shared taxis, known as louages, offer cost-effective travel between Tunis and nearby cities.

Travelers wishing to save money should consider eating where locals eat, bargaining in the souks, and booking accommodation outside peak tourist seasons. Exploring the Medina and its markets is virtually free, aside from the temptation to purchase souvenirs. Cultural sites such as Carthage and the Bardo Museum have modest entry fees, and combination tickets can sometimes provide additional savings. For budget-conscious travelers, Tunis offers an exceptional balance of quality experiences at relatively low costs.

2.3 Safety, Health and Traveler Advice

Tunis is generally a safe destination for tourists, though like any major city, it requires awareness and common sense. Petty crime, such as pickpocketing, can occur in crowded areas, especially in markets or on public transport. Travelers are advised to keep valuables secure, avoid carrying large amounts of cash, and remain attentive in busy environments. Violent crime against tourists is rare, and most visitors report feeling comfortable throughout their stay.

Women traveling alone may experience unwanted attention, but this is typically limited to verbal remarks. Modest clothing, particularly when visiting religious or traditional areas, can help minimize unwanted interactions. Travelers should also respect local customs, especially in more conservative neighborhoods. While Tunis is relatively liberal compared to rural areas, public displays of affection are best avoided, and modesty is appreciated.

Health standards in Tunis are improving, with hospitals and clinics in the capital offering decent levels of care.

Private clinics tend to provide faster service and higher standards compared to public facilities. Travelers should ensure they have adequate travel insurance covering both medical treatment and evacuation, as the cost of care can rise quickly without coverage. Pharmacies are widely available and well stocked, though bringing a personal supply of essential medications is recommended.

Tap water in Tunis is generally safe for residents, but visitors may prefer bottled water to avoid stomach upsets, particularly when first adjusting to local food and drink. Food hygiene standards are variable, so it is best to eat freshly cooked meals and avoid raw or undercooked meat and seafood. Street food is a highlight of Tunisian cuisine, but choose stalls with a high turnover of customers to ensure freshness.

2.4 Emergency Numbers and Services in Tunis

Being aware of emergency numbers and services in Tunis can be reassuring and invaluable during unexpected situations. Tunisia has a centralized system for most emergencies, and calls are typically answered in Arabic and French, though some operators may also understand basic English.

The general emergency number in Tunisia is 197, which connects you directly to the police. This number should be used to report crimes, theft, or any situation requiring police intervention. For medical emergencies, travelers should dial 190 for an ambulance. The fire brigade can be reached at 198 in the event of a fire or rescue situation. These numbers are free to call from any phone within Tunisia.

In addition to emergency services, it is helpful to know the location of your country's embassy or consulate in Tunis. They can provide assistance in cases of lost passports, legal issues, or major emergencies. Many embassies also keep lists of recommended doctors, hospitals, and lawyers.

Taxis in Tunis are widely available and can also be used in urgent, non-life-threatening situations, such as reaching a hospital quickly. Ride-hailing services are emerging in the city, though they are not yet as widespread as in other international destinations. Tourists are encouraged to keep a list of emergency contacts, including their hotel, tour operator, and local friends if applicable, to make response times faster during an unforeseen situation.

Being informed about how to handle emergencies gives travelers peace of mind, ensuring that their focus remains on experiencing the beauty and culture of Tunis rather than worrying about unexpected difficulties.

3. Getting to Tunis

For centuries, Tunis has stood as a gateway to North Africa and the Mediterranean, and today it is more accessible than ever for international travelers. Whether you arrive by plane, train, road, or sea, the city offers multiple entry points that suit different styles of travel. Each mode of transport brings its own charm and considerations, and understanding them will make your arrival in Tunis smoother and more enjoyable.

3.1 By Air: Tunis–Carthage International Airport & Flights

Most international visitors begin their Tunisian journey at Tunis–Carthage International Airport, the primary hub

of the country. Located only about eight kilometers northeast of the city center, it provides travelers with the convenience of quick transfers into Tunis. Despite its relatively compact size compared to larger global airports, Tunis–Carthage handles millions of passengers each year, making it a vital hub for North Africa.

Airlines from Europe, the Middle East, and Africa operate frequent flights to Tunis, with direct routes from major cities such as Paris, Rome, Frankfurt, Istanbul, and Cairo. Seasonal connections also bring visitors from further afield, including charter flights from the UK and Scandinavia during peak summer months. Tunisair, the national carrier, offers reliable service and often the widest network of routes into the city, while international airlines like Lufthansa, Air France, Turkish Airlines, and Emirates also serve the airport.

Upon arrival, travelers will find facilities such as currency exchange offices, ATMs, car rental desks, cafés, and duty-free shops. While the airport is functional, it is recommended to be patient, as queues at passport control and baggage claim can sometimes be lengthy, particularly during busy travel periods. From the airport, taxis are plentiful and provide the easiest means of reaching downtown Tunis in about 20 minutes, depending on traffic. It is advisable to agree on a price before setting off or ensure the meter is switched on. For those who prefer more structured transfers, pre-arranged shuttles and private drivers can be booked in advance.

3.2 By Train: National and Regional Routes

Although Tunis is not directly connected to other countries by train, it remains well-served by Tunisia's national rail network, making train travel a comfortable and scenic way to reach the capital from within the country. The Société Nationale des Chemins de Fer Tunisiens (SNCFT) operates services linking Tunis to coastal cities, interior towns, and key destinations such as Sousse, Sfax, and Gabès.

The main train station in Tunis, Gare de Tunis Ville, sits in the heart of the modern city and serves as a central hub. Trains are an excellent option for travelers arriving from southern or central Tunisia who want to avoid long bus rides. The journeys are not only affordable but also offer glimpses into the Tunisian landscape rolling hills, olive groves, coastal views, and desert outskirts. First- and second-class tickets are available, with first-class offering more comfort at still modest prices.

A particularly scenic route is the train journey along the coast from Sousse to Tunis, which offers travelers stunning views of the Mediterranean. The reliability of trains is generally good, though they may occasionally run behind schedule. For travelers already exploring Tunisia before heading to the capital, the train network is an efficient and enjoyable way to arrive.

3.3 By Bus or Car: Road Trips and Driving Tips

Traveling to Tunis by road offers flexibility and the chance to discover more of Tunisia's regional charm. Long-distance buses are operated by companies such as SNTRI (Société Nationale de Transport Interurbain) and private operators, connecting Tunis with nearly every town and city in the country. The buses depart from major terminals like the Bab Alioua Bus Station, located just outside the Medina. They are budget-friendly, fairly reliable, and offer a good choice for travelers seeking affordability without sacrificing comfort.

For a faster and more localized option, louages shared minibuses or taxis are a quintessential Tunisian experience. Louages leave when full, usually seating around seven to ten passengers, and operate on set routes from regional towns directly to Tunis. They are faster than buses, often cheaper, and provide travelers with an authentic slice of Tunisian life. The main louage station in Tunis is located near Bab Alioua, making it convenient for arrivals into the city.

For those who prefer the independence of driving, renting a car is another option. The Tunisian road network is generally in good condition, especially the highways linking Tunis with coastal cities like Hammamet, Sousse, and Sfax. A self-drive trip allows travelers to explore smaller villages, hidden beaches, and countryside landscapes at their own pace before arriving in Tunis. Driving in Tunisia, however, requires caution—traffic in Tunis itself can be hectic, with a mix of cars, scooters, and pedestrians all sharing the road. Defensive driving and patience are essential, particularly during peak hours. Gas stations are widespread, and fuel is relatively inexpensive compared to many European countries. Road signage is usually in Arabic and French, so having a GPS or a good offline map app is recommended.

3.4 By Sea: Ferries and Mediterranean Cruise Options

For travelers who prefer to arrive by water, Tunis offers an attractive alternative through ferry connections and cruise stops. The Port of La Goulette, located about 11 kilometers northeast of downtown Tunis, is the primary maritime gateway to the city. It is especially popular with European visitors, as several ferry companies operate regular routes linking Tunis with cities in Italy and France. Ferries from Genoa, Marseille, and Palermo are among the most commonly used, and the journeys, though longer than flights, offer the romance of sea travel and the convenience of bringing a car along for extended road trips in Tunisia.

Onboard ferry services typically include cabins, lounges, restaurants, and entertainment, making them comfortable for overnight travel. Prices are competitive, particularly for families or groups who may save money by combining passage with vehicle transport.

Tunis is also a favored stop on Mediterranean cruise itineraries. Major cruise lines frequently include La Goulette in their schedules, allowing visitors to experience the highlights of Tunis, Carthage, and Sidi Bou Said during shore excursions. For cruise passengers, organized tours are the most straightforward way to make the most of a limited time in port, though independent travelers can also take taxis or local transport from La Goulette into the city center.

Arriving by sea offers a unique perspective of Tunis sailing into the bay, with the whitewashed houses of Sidi Bou Said perched above and the ruins of ancient Carthage nearby, is a breathtaking introduction to the capital.

4. Getting Around Tunis

Tunis is a city that invites exploration, whether through its bustling historic Medina, the wide boulevards of the Ville Nouvelle, or the coastal suburbs that line the Mediterranean. Understanding how to move around the city is essential for travelers who want to balance convenience, comfort, and authenticity. Tunis offers a diverse transportation system that combines modern infrastructure with traditional modes of travel unique to Tunisia. From metro lines and buses to shared taxis, walking tours, and cycling routes, getting around Tunis can be an adventure in itself.

4.1 Public Transport: Metro, Buses, and Shared Taxis (Louages)

Public transportation is at the heart of daily life in Tunis, and for travelers, it offers an affordable and authentic way to experience the city. The most prominent system is the Tunis Metro (Métro léger de Tunis), a light rail network that links the city center with surrounding suburbs such as La Marsa, Ariana, and El Mourouj. It is a convenient choice for visiting areas beyond the Medina, especially during peak hours when road traffic can be heavy. Trains are generally reliable, though they can become crowded, particularly in the mornings and evenings when locals commute to work or school. Tickets are inexpensive, making the metro a budget-friendly option for visitors.

The bus system in Tunis covers nearly every district, from the central neighborhoods to the outskirts of the city. Operated by Transtu, buses provide extensive coverage, but they can be less predictable in terms of scheduling and comfort. They are best suited for adventurous travelers who want to immerse themselves in the daily rhythm of Tunisian life. Routes and stops are not always clearly marked in English, so it helps to confirm directions with locals or use mobile apps for guidance. Despite occasional challenges, buses remain the cheapest way to get around the city.

No discussion of Tunisian public transport is complete without mentioning louages, the shared taxis that are a staple of Tunisian mobility. Louages are minibuses or vans that operate on fixed routes but do not depart until they are full. They are extremely popular for intercity travel but are also used for short trips around Tunis and its surrounding suburbs. Louages are recognized by their distinct colored stripes each color representing a different type of route (blue for suburban, red for intercity, yellow for regional). They are faster than buses and slightly more expensive, but still affordable. For many travelers, riding in a louage is a quintessential Tunisian experience, offering a glimpse into local life as passengers from all walks of society share the journey.

4.2 Taxis, Rideshares and Car Rentals

Taxis in Tunis are plentiful and relatively inexpensive compared to many other capital cities. Recognizable by their bright yellow color, they operate both during the day and late into the night. Official taxis are metered, and it is important to ensure that the driver uses the meter to avoid overcharging. Short rides within the city are affordable, while longer trips to areas like La Marsa or Carthage remain reasonable. Taxis are particularly useful for travelers carrying luggage or when moving around after public transport hours.

Ridesharing apps have begun to make an impact in Tunis as well, with services like Bolt and local alternatives offering a convenient and often more reliable way to secure transportation. These apps allow travelers to avoid language barriers and agree on a fare upfront, reducing the risk of misunderstandings. Rideshares are especially useful for visitors unfamiliar with the city's layout or those traveling late at night.

For travelers who wish to explore beyond the city at their own pace, car rentals are widely available. International rental agencies as well as local providers operate in Tunis, particularly around the airport and downtown. Driving in Tunis, however, requires patience and confidence. Traffic can be chaotic, parking is not always easy to find, and local driving habits may seem aggressive to newcomers. That said, renting a car becomes highly practical for day trips to destinations such as Dougga, Zaghouan, or Cap Bon, which are difficult to reach by public transport. It provides freedom and flexibility for those who prefer to set their own itinerary.

4.3 Walking Tours and Cycling Routes in Tunis

Walking remains one of the most rewarding ways to explore Tunis. The Medina, with its narrow alleyways and car-free streets, is best experienced on foot. Here, every step reveals hidden courtyards, ornate doorways, and lively souks where artisans sell their crafts. Guided walking tours are available and highly recommended for first-time visitors, as knowledgeable guides can bring centuries of history to life with stories and insights. Even beyond the Medina, districts like the Ville Nouvelle with its French-style boulevards or Sidi Bou Said with its iconic blue-and-white charm are best enjoyed slowly, without the rush of vehicles.

Cycling in Tunis is less common compared to walking, but it is gradually becoming more accessible as bike rentals and organized tours gain popularity. The seaside suburb of La Marsa and the scenic routes toward

Gammarth and Carthage offer particularly pleasant cycling experiences. Coastal roads provide fresh air and stunning views of the Mediterranean, making cycling a relaxing way to combine exploration with exercise. Within the city center, cycling can be more challenging due to traffic congestion, but certain wide avenues and quieter neighborhoods are manageable for confident cyclists. In recent years, efforts have been made to promote eco-friendly transport, and new bike paths are slowly being developed. For adventurous travelers, cycling adds a unique and memorable perspective to their exploration of Tunis.

4.4 Insider Tips for Moving Around Like a Local

To truly navigate Tunis like a local, travelers need to embrace both the efficiency and the unpredictability of the city's transport system. One important tip is to always carry small change, as public transport tickets and short taxi rides are inexpensive and drivers often cannot break large bills. When using taxis, it is customary to greet the driver and confirm the destination clearly before starting the ride. For louages, be prepared to wait until the vehicle fills up, but also enjoy the opportunity to observe the social interactions that unfold inside.

Locals often mix different modes of transport in a single day, taking the metro for longer distances, taxis for shorter trips, and walking when navigating crowded areas. Adopting this flexible approach can help travelers save time and money. Avoid peak rush hours if possible, as metro trains and buses can become uncomfortably crowded. On the other hand, walking in the early morning or evening provides a chance to see the city in its most authentic moments, with markets opening or families gathering for evening strolls.

Travelers should also take advantage of mobile apps, which are becoming increasingly useful in Tunis. Apps for taxis and rideshares simplify communication, while mapping tools help navigate bus and metro routes. Asking locals for directions is common and often welcomed, as Tunisians are known for their hospitality and willingness to assist visitors.

Above all, patience and curiosity are essential. Transportation in Tunis is not always about speed or convenience it is often about the experience itself. Whether sharing laughs with strangers in a louage, sipping tea after a long walk through the Medina, or watching the sea roll by from a train window, moving around Tunis is as much a part of the journey as the destinations themselves.

5. Where to Stay in Tunis

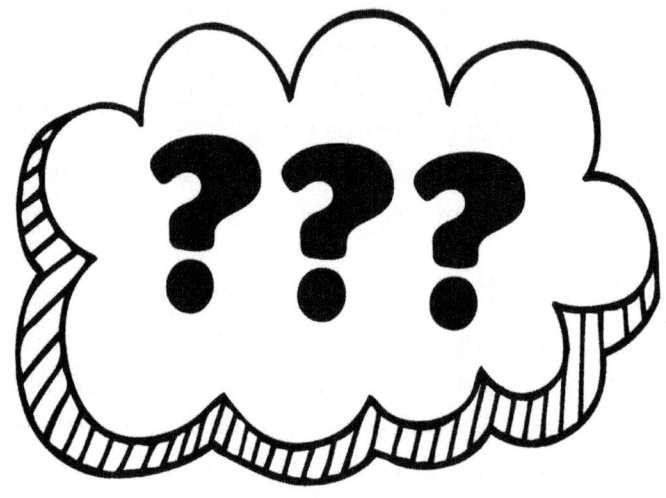

Choosing where to stay in Tunis is an important part of shaping the traveler's experience. The city offers a wide variety of accommodation options that suit every kind of visitor, from luxury seekers looking for refined elegance and Mediterranean views to budget-conscious travelers seeking comfort and value. Tunis also boasts an exciting range of unique stays, from traditional Tunisian houses known as dars to boutique hotels that combine heritage with modern design. Beyond the types of accommodations, location plays a key role. Each neighborhood in Tunis offers a different atmosphere, from the historic charm of the Medina to the coastal serenity of La Marsa and Carthage. Knowing the options in detail helps travelers make the right choice for their journey.

5.1 Luxury Hotels and Resorts

Tunis has an impressive selection of luxury hotels and resorts that cater to travelers who want to enjoy comfort, style, and impeccable service. These properties often combine international standards with a distinctly Tunisian flair. Many luxury hotels are located either in the modern city center or in the northern coastal suburbs such as Gammarth, Carthage, and La Marsa, where the Mediterranean shoreline creates a scenic backdrop.

Luxury hotels in Tunis typically feature spacious rooms with panoramic views, fine dining restaurants that highlight both international and Tunisian cuisine, and wellness facilities such as spas, hammams, and swimming pools. Some of the resorts along the coast offer private beach access, making them ideal for travelers who want a mix of cultural exploration in the city and seaside relaxation. Guests can expect attentive staff, high-end amenities, and a setting that reflects both the historical grandeur and the contemporary energy of the capital. These accommodations are well-suited for business travelers, honeymooners, or anyone who wants to experience Tunis with a touch of indulgence.

5.2 Mid-Range and Budget-Friendly Options

For travelers who want comfort without overspending, Tunis offers a wide variety of mid-range hotels and budget-friendly stays. Many of these accommodations are conveniently located in and around the city center, providing easy access to public transportation, major attractions, and dining options. Mid-range hotels in Tunis usually provide clean and comfortable rooms, reliable services such as Wi-Fi and breakfast, and friendly staff who are accustomed to international visitors. They are often modern in style, though some incorporate Tunisian decorative elements to give travelers a sense of local charm.

Budget-friendly hotels, hostels, and guesthouses are also available for those traveling on a tighter budget. These establishments may not offer the same level of luxury or extensive facilities as upscale properties, but they make up for it with affordability and a sense of authenticity. Travelers who stay in budget accommodations often find themselves in closer contact with locals, whether through family-run establishments or shared facilities where fellow travelers connect. These options are especially attractive for backpackers, students, and those planning longer stays. Despite being affordable, many of these budget-friendly places still prioritize cleanliness, safety, and convenience.

5.3 Boutique Hotels, Guesthouses, and Traditional Dar Stays

One of the most memorable ways to experience Tunis is by staying in boutique hotels, guesthouses, or restored traditional houses known as dars. These accommodations offer a unique perspective on Tunisian culture and history, often blending heritage with contemporary comfort. Boutique hotels are typically smaller in size than luxury resorts, but they stand out for

their carefully designed interiors, personalized service, and charming atmospheres. Many are located in the Medina or in historic neighborhoods, where centuries-old architecture has been transformed into stylish places to stay.

Guesthouses provide a homier experience, with warm hospitality and opportunities to connect with Tunisian hosts. They are ideal for travelers who appreciate a more personal touch rather than the formality of larger hotels. Traditional dar stays, meanwhile, immerse travelers directly into Tunisian heritage. Dars are historic houses built around central courtyards, often decorated with colorful tiles, ornate doors, and detailed plasterwork. Renovated dars combine the elegance of old architecture with modern conveniences, allowing visitors to sleep in spaces that once belonged to Tunisian aristocrats or merchants. These unique stays allow guests not only to rest but also to feel a part of the living history of Tunis.

5.4 Neighborhood Guide: Medina, La Marsa, Carthage, and Beyond

Deciding where to stay in Tunis is not just about the type of accommodation but also about the neighborhood. Each area of the city offers a different experience, and travelers should consider what kind of atmosphere best suits their trip.

The Medina of Tunis is the historic heart of the city and perfect for those who want to immerse themselves in culture and history. Staying in the Medina means waking up to the sounds of traditional markets, wandering through winding alleyways, and being within walking distance of mosques, palaces, and artisan workshops. The accommodations here are often boutique hotels or traditional dars, offering an authentic yet atmospheric stay.

La Marsa, located to the north of the city, is known for its seaside charm. It is popular with both locals and visitors who want to enjoy the beach while still having access to restaurants, cafés, and a lively social scene. Accommodations here range from boutique hotels with sea views to luxury resorts that make the most of the Mediterranean coastline.

Carthage offers a quieter and more historical setting. Known for its ancient ruins and elegant villas, it appeals to travelers who want both cultural exploration and tranquility. Staying in Carthage provides easy access to archaeological sites while still being close to the coast.

Gammarth, another coastal suburb, is especially popular for its luxury resorts and high-end hotels. This area is well-suited for travelers looking for beach relaxation, spa treatments, and premium services, while still being a short drive from the city center.

For those who prefer convenience and modernity, the Ville Nouvelle or downtown area of Tunis offers hotels that are close to business centers, shopping streets, and public transport. It is a practical base for business travelers or tourists who want to be centrally located.

Together, these neighborhoods create a diverse map of accommodation choices. From the historical magic of the Medina to the cosmopolitan energy of La Marsa and the calm refinement of Carthage, Tunis provides a variety of options that ensure every traveler can find the right place to stay.

6. Exploring Tunis

Exploring Tunis is a journey through time, culture, and everyday life. The city is a living museum where ancient ruins, medieval Islamic architecture, colonial boulevards, and modern art spaces all coexist. Travelers will quickly notice that Tunis cannot be defined by one single identity; instead, it is a mosaic of influences that have shaped it over centuries. This makes exploration an endlessly rewarding experience whether you are wandering through its centuries-old Medina, climbing over Roman ruins, or sipping coffee in a hidden café by the sea.

In this chapter, we will cover the most important attractions that no traveler should miss, the hidden gems that often escape the average visitor's eye, and carefully curated itineraries that help you make the most of your time in the capital. Tunis can be overwhelming at first glance, but with the right guidance, it reveals itself as one of the most fascinating capitals in North Africa.

6.1 Top Attractions: Medina of Tunis, Carthage, Bardo Museum and More

The most iconic starting point for any journey through Tunis is the Medina of Tunis. This historic quarter, a UNESCO World Heritage Site, is a maze of narrow alleyways, bustling souks, and centuries-old mosques. The Medina is more than a collection of historic monuments; it is a living neighborhood where generations of families have lived and traded. Here, travelers will find the Zitouna Mosque, one of the oldest and most significant mosques in Tunisia, surrounded by madrassas, hammams, and caravanserais. Each corner reveals artisan shops selling everything from handmade carpets to intricately worked jewelry. Exploring the Medina is an immersion into Tunisian daily life, where the past and present merge seamlessly.

Just beyond the Medina lies Carthage, the legendary city once rival to Rome. Though much of the ancient city was destroyed, its ruins still stand as a testament to one of history's greatest civilizations. Visitors can explore the Antonine Baths, the Punic Ports, and the Carthage Museum, all set against the stunning backdrop of the Mediterranean. Carthage is not only about its archaeological sites but also about its atmosphere. It is a place where history breathes through every stone, reminding travelers of the power and fragility of empires.

Another unmissable stop is the Bardo National Museum, home to one of the world's largest collections of Roman mosaics. Located in a former Ottoman palace, the museum showcases Tunisia's vast history, from Carthaginian artifacts to Islamic art. The Bardo is more than a museum; it is a journey through Tunisia's layered identity, showing how diverse cultures have left their imprint on this land.

Beyond these highlights, Tunis offers many more attractions that reflect its multifaceted character. The Avenue Habib Bourguiba, often compared to the Champs-Élysées in Paris, is the heart of the modern city with its cafés, theaters, and colonial architecture. For those seeking a taste of spirituality, the Cathedral of St. Vincent de Paul stands as a reminder of the French colonial era and the coexistence of cultures in Tunis. Together, these attractions form the essential foundation for understanding the city.

6.2 Hidden Gems: Street Art, Secret Cafés and Lesser-Known Sites

While the top attractions provide the backbone of a visit to Tunis, the city's true charm often lies in its hidden corners. One such discovery is the street art scene, particularly in neighborhoods like Lafayette and parts of the Medina. Colorful murals cover old buildings, reflecting the voice of Tunisia's youth and their hopes for the future. These works of art transform ordinary walls into canvases of expression, offering travelers an unexpected glimpse into the city's modern identity.

Equally enchanting are the secret cafés scattered across Tunis. In the Medina, tucked behind unmarked doors, visitors may stumble upon traditional cafés where men sip strong coffee or mint tea while playing chess. Outside the old town, in neighborhoods like La Marsa and Sidi Bou Said, chic modern cafés offer stunning sea views and attract a younger crowd. These places are not always easy to find, but they reward the curious traveler with a sense of belonging to the local rhythm of life.

Among the lesser-known sites, the Tourbet El Bey Mausoleum is worth visiting. This Ottoman-era tomb complex houses the remains of princes and dignitaries, decorated with ornate tilework and carved wood. Unlike the crowded Zitouna Mosque, this site often sees few tourists, allowing for a quieter, more reflective experience. Another gem is the Belvedere Park, a sprawling green space where families gather on weekends and where visitors can enjoy panoramic views of the city. The park also contains the Tunis Zoo, a favorite for locals but often overlooked by international travelers.

For those who enjoy blending history with discovery, the Kasbah Square and surrounding government buildings offer a fascinating glimpse into Tunisia's political life. While not as grand as the Medina or Carthage, these areas give travelers context about Tunisia's modern story. These hidden gems add depth to a visit, moving beyond the postcard images and inviting travelers to engage with Tunis on a more personal level.

6.3 Suggested Itineraries (1-Day, 3-Day and 5-Day Plans)

For travelers short on time, a one-day itinerary focuses on the essentials. Start in the Medina with a guided walk through its souks, stopping at Zitouna Mosque and the Kasbah. Pause for lunch at a traditional restaurant tucked inside an old palace, then spend the afternoon at the Bardo National Museum. End your day with a stroll down Avenue Habib Bourguiba, where you can enjoy dinner at a modern Tunisian fusion restaurant before experiencing the city's nightlife.

For a three-day stay, expand your exploration to include Carthage and Sidi Bou Said. Dedicate your second day to Carthage's ruins, visiting the Antonine Baths, the Byrsa Hill, and the Carthage Museum. In the evening, head to Sidi Bou Said, where whitewashed houses with blue doors glow under the setting sun, offering a perfect backdrop for dinner with a sea view. On the third day, explore the Ville Nouvelle, admire colonial architecture, and spend time in the Belvedere Park. For something unique, seek out one of Tunis's hidden cafés for a quiet afternoon before departing.

A five-day plan allows for a more immersive experience. In addition to the highlights of the first three days, travelers can dedicate a full day to exploring the wider suburbs of Tunis, such as La Marsa with its sandy beaches or Gammarth, known for its resorts and seaside dining. A final day can be reserved for off-the-beaten-path adventures, such as visiting the ruins of Dougga on a day trip, or joining a cooking class in the Medina to learn the secrets of Tunisian cuisine. This extended itinerary provides a balance between history, leisure, and cultural immersion.

Exploring Tunis is never about ticking boxes on a sightseeing list. It is about connecting with a city that thrives on contrasts: ancient ruins and contemporary art, bustling souks and quiet gardens, monumental museums and hidden corners. Each traveler experiences Tunis differently, but all leave with the memory of a city that reveals itself slowly, layer by layer, like a story waiting to be told.

7. Experiencing Local Culture

Tunis is not just the capital of Tunisia; it is the beating heart of the nation's identity. To truly understand the city, visitors must look beyond its historic landmarks and into the living culture that defines daily life. The charm of Tunis lies in the way traditions blend with modern influences, where centuries-old practices continue alongside contemporary trends. Experiencing the local culture of Tunis is more than sightseeing it is about immersing yourself in its rhythm, its flavors, its artistry, and its celebrations.

7.1 Tunisian Traditions, Etiquette and Lifestyle

Tunisians are known for their warmth and hospitality, and in Tunis this is deeply embedded in the city's social fabric. Visitors are often welcomed with open arms, offered mint tea or coffee as a gesture of friendship. Hospitality is not just a custom but a point of pride, and it extends beyond homes into shops, cafés, and markets.

Religion plays an important role in everyday life, with Islam shaping social norms and practices. The call to prayer echoes across Tunis several times a day, and during the holy month of Ramadan, daily routines adjust to fasting and nightly gatherings for iftar meals. Visitors are not expected to participate in religious practices but should be respectful, especially when visiting mosques or traditional neighborhoods. Modest clothing is appreciated, particularly in conservative areas or religious sites, though in cosmopolitan districts like La Marsa or Sidi Bou Said the dress code is more relaxed.

Etiquette in Tunis places a strong emphasis on politeness. A handshake is the most common greeting between men, while between men and women, greetings vary depending on comfort levels; a nod or verbal greeting may replace physical contact. It is customary to greet with "As-salamu alaykum" (peace be upon you) and respond with "Wa alaykum as-salam." Bargaining is expected in souks, but always done with good humor and respect. Social life in Tunis often revolves around family, food, and community, with gatherings frequently stretching long into the night over shared meals and conversations.

The Tunisian lifestyle balances work with leisure in a way that emphasizes connection. In the mornings, you might find people hurrying through the Ville Nouvelle for work, but by afternoon and evening, cafés fill with locals sipping espresso or mint tea, smoking shisha, and watching football matches on television. Life here is as much about social interaction as it is about productivity. This rhythm is one of the most endearing aspects of Tunis time is valued, but people are valued more.

7.2 Culinary Journey: Food, Drinks and Street Eats in Tunis

Tunis is a culinary treasure trove that reflects the influences of the Mediterranean, the Arab world, and North Africa, all while carrying its own unique flavors. Food is an essential part of Tunisian culture, and eating is never just about sustenance it is an act of celebration and community.

The backbone of Tunisian cuisine is couscous, often prepared with lamb, chicken, or fresh seafood, and enriched with vegetables and a fiery harissa sauce. Harissa, the famous chili paste, is not just a condiment but a cultural symbol. It appears on nearly every table, adding depth and spice to countless dishes. In Tunis, couscous with fish is a local favorite, often enjoyed along the coast where the catch of the day makes its way directly from the sea to the plate.

Street food is another highlight of the Tunisian culinary journey. The bustling streets of Tunis offer savory snacks like brik, a thin pastry filled with egg, tuna, and parsley, fried to golden perfection. Fricassé, a fried sandwich stuffed with potatoes, olives, harissa, and tuna, is beloved by locals as a quick and hearty bite. Sweet lovers will find joy in pastries such as bambalouni, Tunisian-style doughnuts dusted with sugar, often enjoyed with tea in seaside cafés.

Beverages are just as important to Tunisian culture. Mint tea, often served with pine nuts floating on top, is a staple of hospitality and social gatherings. Strong espresso is equally popular, a legacy of French influence, and is part of the daily rhythm of life. Freshly squeezed orange juice, pomegranate juice, and date-based drinks add a refreshing touch to the Tunisian table.

The culinary journey is not complete without exploring traditional restaurants, where meals are often multi-course feasts beginning with mezze-style appetizers, followed by hearty stews, grilled meats, or seafood dishes, and ending with sweet pastries drenched in honey and nuts. Dining in Tunis is not only about food it is about the experience of sharing, lingering, and connecting.

7.3 Festivals and Cultural Celebrations in 2026

Tunis comes alive through its festivals and cultural events, which bring together tradition, art, music, and community. These celebrations offer travelers a chance to witness the city at its most vibrant and joyful.

One of the most important cultural observances is Ramadan, followed by Eid al-Fitr, when the city bursts into celebration with family feasts, new clothes, and gatherings that light up neighborhoods. Eid al-Adha is another significant festival, marked with rituals, generosity, and communal meals. While these are religious in nature, visitors are always welcome to share in the atmosphere of unity and festivity.

Beyond religious holidays, Tunis hosts a wide range of cultural events. The Carthage International Festival, held every summer in the ancient Roman amphitheater of Carthage, is one of North Africa's premier music and performing arts festivals. It attracts artists from across the globe and offers unforgettable performances under the stars. The Medina Festival brings traditional music, theater, and dance into the heart of Tunis's old city, making its historic alleys resonate with cultural expression.

In 2026, new art exhibitions, film festivals, and culinary fairs are expected to add even more dynamism to Tunis's cultural calendar. These events reflect the city's growing position as a cultural hub in the region, bridging Africa, the Arab world, and Europe. For travelers, attending a festival in Tunis is more than entertainment—it is a window into the soul of the city.

7.4 Shopping: Souks, Handicrafts and Modern Boutiques

No visit to Tunis is complete without exploring its markets and shops. Shopping here is not merely a transaction but an experience of history, craftsmanship, and artistry.

The souks of the Medina are a maze of colors, scents, and sounds, where merchants sell everything from handwoven carpets to silver jewelry, leather goods, ceramics, and traditional clothing. Each souk tends to specialize in certain products: Souk el-Attarine for perfumes and spices, Souk des Chechias for traditional woolen caps, and Souk el-Birka for jewelry. Bargaining is expected and part of the fun, but always approached with friendliness and patience.

Handicrafts are among the most cherished purchases for travelers. Tunis is known for its intricate mosaics, pottery decorated with traditional motifs, and finely embroidered textiles. Artisans often pass their skills down through generations, and buying their work helps preserve these traditions. Leather goods, from slippers to bags, are also popular, combining practicality with authentic Tunisian design.

For those looking for a more modern shopping experience, Tunis offers stylish boutiques and shopping centers. Areas such as La Marsa and Berges du Lac feature contemporary fashion brands, art galleries, and concept stores that cater to a younger, trendier crowd. Here, traditional influences often meet modern design, creating unique blends that appeal to international tastes.

Whether you're hunting for souvenirs, luxury items, or simply enjoying the atmosphere of bustling marketplaces, shopping in Tunis connects you directly to its people and culture. Each item carries a story, each purchase supports a tradition, and each market visit becomes a memory.

8. Activities and Adventures Around Tunis

Tunis is not only a city of history and culture but also a vibrant hub for activities and adventures that allow visitors to experience the richness of Tunisia in many forms. The capital is ideally located between the Mediterranean Sea, fertile plains, and historic sites, making it a perfect base for day trips, outdoor pursuits, and cultural explorations. Travelers looking for adventure will find a wealth of options, from exploring ancient ruins to strolling along picturesque coastal villages, from enjoying a lively nightlife to unwinding in hammams that continue centuries-old traditions. Tunis offers something for every mood and every traveler, whether the preference is for discovery, relaxation, or entertainment.

8.1 Day Trips and Excursions: Sidi Bou Said, Dougga, Hammamet and More

Tunis is surrounded by a number of remarkable destinations that can be reached within a short drive or train ride, making day trips a highlight of any stay. Perhaps the most famous is Sidi Bou Said, a cliff-top village overlooking the Mediterranean. Known for its striking blue-and-white architecture, winding cobbled lanes, and breathtaking sea views, Sidi Bou Said is a destination that has inspired countless artists and writers. Travelers can enjoy walking through its streets, visiting art galleries, sipping mint tea at the iconic Café des Nattes, and shopping for handicrafts such as ceramics and jewelry.

For those who wish to delve into Tunisia's ancient past, Dougga is an unmissable excursion. Located about two hours from Tunis, Dougga is one of the best-preserved Roman towns in North Africa and a UNESCO World Heritage Site. Visitors can wander among its theaters, temples, baths, and forums, all set against a scenic backdrop of rolling hills and olive groves. Unlike many crowded archaeological sites, Dougga retains a peaceful atmosphere where history can be absorbed at a leisurely pace.

Closer to Tunis is Carthage, the legendary city that was once Rome's great rival. The ruins of Carthage are scattered across several districts near the capital, and while not as intact as Dougga, they carry immense historical significance. Highlights include the Antonine Baths, the Roman amphitheater, and the Punic ports. Pairing Carthage with a visit to the Bardo Museum offers a complete journey through Tunisia's ancient heritage.

Another popular getaway is Hammamet, a coastal town known for its beaches, resorts, and historic medina. Just over an hour's drive from Tunis, Hammamet is a place to combine leisure with exploration. The town's sandy beaches are ideal for swimming and sunbathing, while the old town provides a charming setting of narrow streets and seaside views. Hammamet is also famous for its vibrant cultural scene, particularly the International Festival of Hammamet, which hosts music, theater, and dance performances every summer.

Other excursions from Tunis include Nabeul, the capital of pottery and ceramics; Zaghouan, with its Roman aqueduct and mountain landscapes; and the Cap Bon Peninsula, known for citrus groves, fishing villages, and wild coastlines. These destinations provide variety and depth, ensuring that travelers can experience more than just the capital during their visit.

8.2 Beaches and Water Sports Near Tunis

The Mediterranean coast offers abundant opportunities for beach lovers and water sport enthusiasts, and Tunis provides easy access to some of the region's best shorelines. Within the capital itself, La Goulette is the closest beach area, popular with locals for its seafood restaurants and sandy stretches where families gather. While not the most pristine, it offers a taste of authentic Tunisian seaside life.

A short distance away lies Gammarth, a resort area north of Tunis. Gammarth boasts upscale hotels, private beach clubs, and wide sandy beaches that are cleaner and quieter than those in La Goulette. Visitors can relax under parasols, enjoy fresh seafood by the sea, or take part in activities such as jet skiing and sailing. For a more picturesque setting, the coastline near La Marsa offers charming beaches where the atmosphere is youthful and lively, attracting both locals and expatriates.

For those who wish to combine seaside beauty with cultural exploration, Hammamet once again emerges as a prime choice. Its beaches are among the most attractive in Tunisia, with long sandy stretches and calm waters ideal for swimming. Water sports such as windsurfing, parasailing, and banana boat rides are widely available. Diving and snorkeling are also possible, particularly along the Cap Bon Peninsula, where the waters are clearer and marine life more abundant.

Another excellent destination is Korbous, located along the Gulf of Tunis. Unlike typical beach resorts, Korbous is known for its hot springs that flow directly into the sea, offering a unique blend of relaxation and natural wellness. Visitors can enjoy therapeutic baths while overlooking the Mediterranean horizon.

8.3 Nightlife: Cafés, Bars, and Live Music

As the sun sets, Tunis takes on a new rhythm, offering a variety of nightlife experiences that reflect both its modern character and traditional spirit. Unlike the

all-night party scenes of some Mediterranean cities, Tunisian nightlife tends to be more relaxed and social, centered around cafés, live music, and intimate venues.

Cafés are at the heart of Tunisian social life, and in the evenings they fill with people enjoying mint tea, Turkish coffee, or fresh juices. In areas like La Marsa and Sidi Bou Said, traditional cafés offer stunning views of the sea, making them ideal for a laid-back evening. Some of the most iconic include Café des Nattes and Café Sidi Chabaane, both perched high above the Mediterranean and offering an unforgettable atmosphere.

For those seeking more contemporary entertainment, Tunis has a growing number of lounges, bars, and nightclubs, especially in neighborhoods such as Gammarth and Berges du Lac. These venues often feature DJs, cocktails, and modern decor, catering to both locals and international visitors. While alcohol is available in licensed establishments, many nightlife venues remain alcohol-free, focusing instead on live music and social gatherings.

Music is an essential part of Tunisian nightlife, ranging from traditional Andalusian and Malouf performances to jazz, rock, and electronic music. Small theaters and cultural centers in Tunis often host concerts and performances, while summer festivals bring internationally acclaimed artists to stages near the city. The eclectic music scene reflects Tunisia's blend of heritage and modern creativity, making nightlife in Tunis both diverse and engaging.

8.4 Wellness: Hammams, Spas, and Relaxation Spots

For travelers seeking relaxation and rejuvenation, Tunis offers a rich tradition of wellness that combines age-old practices with modern luxury. The hammam, or traditional steam bath, is an integral part of Tunisian culture, rooted in Roman and Arab traditions. Visiting a hammam is not only a cleansing ritual but also a cultural experience, where locals gather to unwind, socialize, and purify body and mind. In the Medina of Tunis, several authentic hammams still operate, offering an atmosphere that feels centuries old. Travelers can immerse

themselves in this experience, often followed by massages and scrubs that leave the body refreshed.

Beyond traditional hammams, Tunis is home to luxury spas located within hotels and resorts, especially in Gammarth and La Marsa. These spas often blend modern treatments with Tunisian-inspired therapies, using natural ingredients such as olive oil, sea salt, and aromatic herbs. Wellness retreats and yoga sessions are becoming increasingly popular, providing a holistic escape from the bustle of city life.

Nature also plays a role in Tunisian wellness. Korbous, mentioned earlier for its hot springs, has long been a destination for therapeutic bathing, drawing visitors who seek healing in its mineral-rich waters. The surrounding hills and coastline create a tranquil environment, ideal for relaxation and contemplation.

For a slower-paced form of wellness, simply strolling along the Mediterranean promenades of La Marsa or enjoying the sunset views in Sidi Bou Said can be restorative. These serene experiences remind visitors that wellness in Tunis is not limited to spas and hammams but is woven into the everyday lifestyle of its people.

9. Practical Information

Traveling to Tunis is a rewarding experience, but as with any destination, having a solid grasp of practical information will make your journey smoother, more enjoyable, and stress-free. Tunis is a city where tradition meets modernity, where Arabic is spoken alongside French, where ancient streets coexist with modern cafés, and where travelers of all backgrounds can feel welcomed if they are equipped with the right knowledge. This section provides everything you need to know about the everyday details that will help you navigate life in Tunis, from language tips and staying connected to cultural etiquette and accessibility considerations.

9.1 Language Guide: Useful Arabic & French Phrases

The official language of Tunisia is Arabic, with Tunisian Arabic (Darija) being the local dialect. However, French is widely spoken due to the country's history as a French protectorate, and many signs, menus, and official documents are bilingual. In the capital city of Tunis, most residents, particularly in the younger generation and in the tourism industry, switch fluidly between Arabic and French. English is less common but is gradually growing, especially among young professionals and in international businesses.

Learning a few key phrases in Arabic and French will go a long way in connecting with locals and showing respect for their culture. Even a simple greeting in Arabic is warmly appreciated.

Common Arabic Phrases in Tunis:

Hello: As-salāmu ʿalaykum (السلام عليكم)

Thank you: Shukran (شكرا)

Yes: Naʿam (نعم)

No: Lā (لا)

How much is this?: B'qaddech? (؟بقداش)

Goodbye: Maʿa as-salāma (مع السلامة)

Common French Phrases in Tunis:

Hello/Good day: Bonjour

Thank you: Merci

Please: S'il vous plaît

Excuse me: Excusez-moi
How much?: Combien ça coûte ?

I don't speak French very well: Je ne parle pas bien français

Most Tunisians will be patient with travelers who make an effort to communicate. Even if you only know a handful of words, using them in daily interactions whether in the Medina's markets, at a café, or in a taxi often leads to friendlier service and warmer smiles.

9.2 Connectivity: Wi-Fi, SIM Cards & Internet in Tunis

Tunis is a modern city where staying connected is relatively easy, but it helps to know your options in advance. Wi-Fi is common in hotels, cafés, and restaurants, particularly in central areas and the more touristic districts like La Marsa and Sidi Bou Said. However, speeds may vary, and in some older establishments, connections can be slow or unstable. For travelers who need reliable internet access, purchasing a local SIM card is the most convenient option.

Tunisia has several major mobile providers, including Tunisie Telecom, Ooredoo, and Orange Tunisia. Each offers prepaid SIM cards that are affordable and widely available at the airport, phone shops, or authorized kiosks. Activation is usually quick, and packages include both calls and generous data bundles, making it easy to navigate the city, use maps, or stay in touch with friends and family abroad.

For travelers who prefer not to change SIM cards, roaming is available but can be expensive, depending on your home network provider. Portable Wi-Fi devices are also an option, though less commonly used compared to SIM cards.

Internet cafés, once popular, have become rare as mobile internet has taken over. Still, you will find them in student areas and neighborhoods where younger crowds gather. Speeds are typically good enough for browsing, messaging, and video calls. Tunis is also expanding its digital infrastructure, meaning that by 2026, connectivity is expected to be faster and more reliable than ever before.

9.3 Do's and Don'ts in Tunisian Culture

Understanding local customs and etiquette is essential when visiting Tunis. Tunisians are generally welcoming and tolerant, but cultural awareness demonstrates respect and will enrich your travel experience. Here are some important do's and don'ts:

Do's:

Greet politely: Always greet with a "Bonjour" in French or "As-salāmu ʿalaykum" in Arabic when entering shops, restaurants, or speaking to locals. Greetings are an important part of Tunisian culture.

Dress modestly in certain places: While Tunis is relatively liberal compared to other parts of the Arab world, modest clothing is appreciated in religious or traditional settings, such as mosques and local neighborhoods.

Use your right hand: When offering or receiving items, the right hand is traditionally used as a sign of respect.

Bargain politely: In souks and markets, haggling is expected. Approach it with patience and a friendly smile rather than aggression.

Don'ts:

Avoid public displays of affection: Hand-holding is acceptable, but kissing or hugging in public is frowned upon, especially in conservative areas.

Don't photograph people without permission: Many locals dislike being photographed, particularly women. Always ask before taking pictures.

Avoid sensitive political discussions: While Tunisians are open to conversation, avoid controversial debates about politics, religion, or personal freedoms unless you know your host well.

Don't assume everyone drinks alcohol: While alcohol is available in many restaurants and bars, not all Tunisians consume it due to religious beliefs. Be mindful and discreet.

By observing these simple do's and don'ts, travelers can enjoy smoother interactions and avoid misunderstandings. Respecting customs not only helps you fit in but also shows gratitude for the hospitality you will undoubtedly encounter.

9.4 Accessibility & Travel Tips for All Travelers

Tunis is a city that continues to develop its infrastructure, but accessibility can vary. Travelers with disabilities may face challenges, especially in historic areas such as the Medina, where narrow alleys, uneven cobblestones, and staircases are common. Sidewalks in some parts of the city are not always well maintained, and curb cuts are inconsistent. However, progress is being made to improve accessibility in newer neighborhoods, public buildings, and modern hotels.

Most international hotels and luxury resorts offer wheelchair access, elevators, and adapted rooms with accessible bathrooms. Major attractions such as the Bardo National Museum and Carthage's archaeological sites are making efforts to improve facilities, though complete accessibility may not always be guaranteed. For travelers requiring special accommodations, it is best to confirm in advance with hotels and tour operators.

Public transportation presents mixed accessibility. The light rail and metro systems are not fully adapted, but buses and newer taxis are more accommodating. Ride-hailing apps provide an additional option for travelers who require more convenience.

Beyond accessibility, general travel tips for all visitors include carrying small denominations of cash for taxis and small shops, staying hydrated in the summer heat, and planning your itinerary with rest periods, especially if exploring the bustling Medina. Tunis is a safe and friendly city, but like any urban center, keeping an eye on personal belongings in crowded areas is advisable.

For solo travelers, Tunis is generally welcoming, with a vibrant café culture that makes it easy to meet people. Women travelers, while safe, may receive unwanted attention in some areas, so modest clothing and confidence in public spaces can help avoid discomfort. Families will find Tunis hospitable, with plenty of activities suitable for children, including beaches, parks, and interactive museums.

In summary, Tunis is a city that can be navigated by all types of travelers, provided they are aware of its cultural norms and infrastructural realities. By preparing with the right knowledge, visitors can enjoy everything from the historic wonders of Carthage to the lively modern neighborhoods with ease and confidence.

10. Traveler's Resources

Traveling to Tunis can be a rewarding and seamless experience when you are equipped with the right resources. While the city offers a wealth of attractions, history, and culture, being well-prepared ensures that you spend less time worrying about logistics and more time enjoying the essence of your journey. From useful apps that simplify navigation to consulate information for peace of mind, traveler resources play an essential role in making any trip smooth and memorable. In Tunis, these resources are widely accessible, and many have been designed with the international visitor in mind. This chapter serves as a complete guide to what travelers need in terms of tools, contacts, and planning essentials for 2026.

10.1 Useful Apps, Maps and Online Tools

In an increasingly digital age, technology can be a traveler's best companion. For navigation in Tunis, smartphone apps such as Google Maps and Maps.me remain indispensable. They allow visitors to pinpoint their location in the Medina's maze-like alleys or find the best route to Carthage or La Marsa. Offline map options are highly recommended, since mobile data may not always be reliable in crowded areas or while traveling outside the city. For those exploring Tunis by public transport, apps that track buses, trams, and the metro provide real-time updates and timetables, saving both time and confusion.

Ridesharing apps such as Bolt and local taxi apps are also widely used in Tunis, offering a safer and more predictable way of getting around compared to hailing a cab from the street. Food delivery apps are convenient for those staying longer or renting apartments, providing easy access to both local specialties and international cuisine. For cultural enrichment, there are mobile guides dedicated to Tunisian history and monuments, some of which use augmented reality to recreate ancient Carthage or provide interactive storytelling while walking through the Medina.

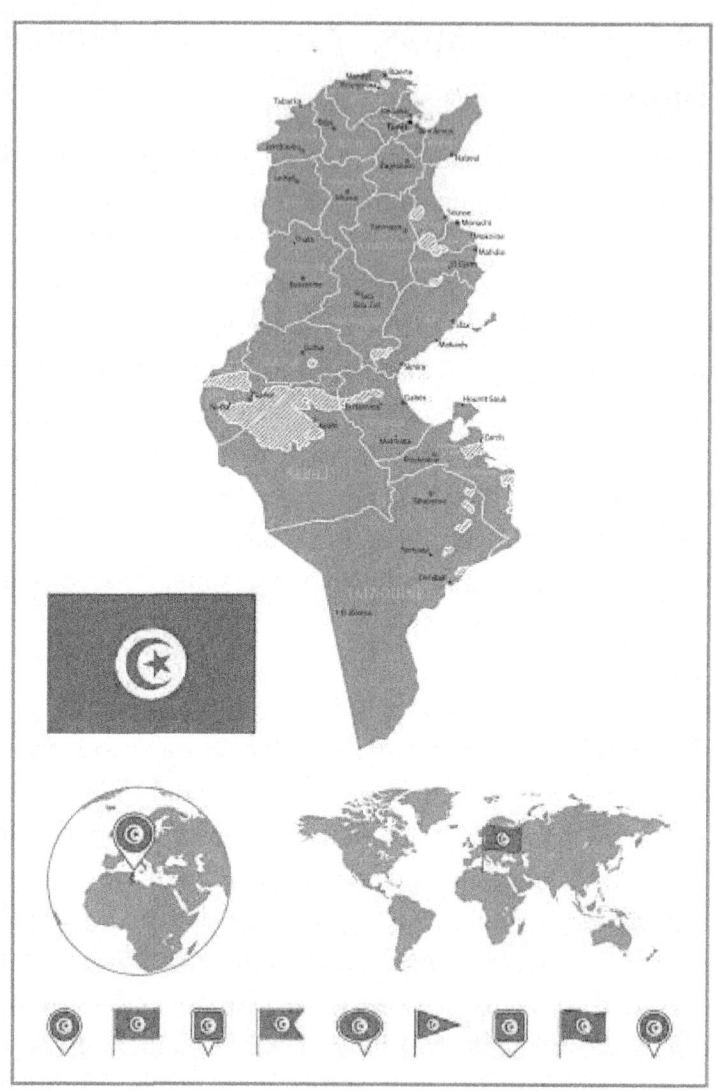

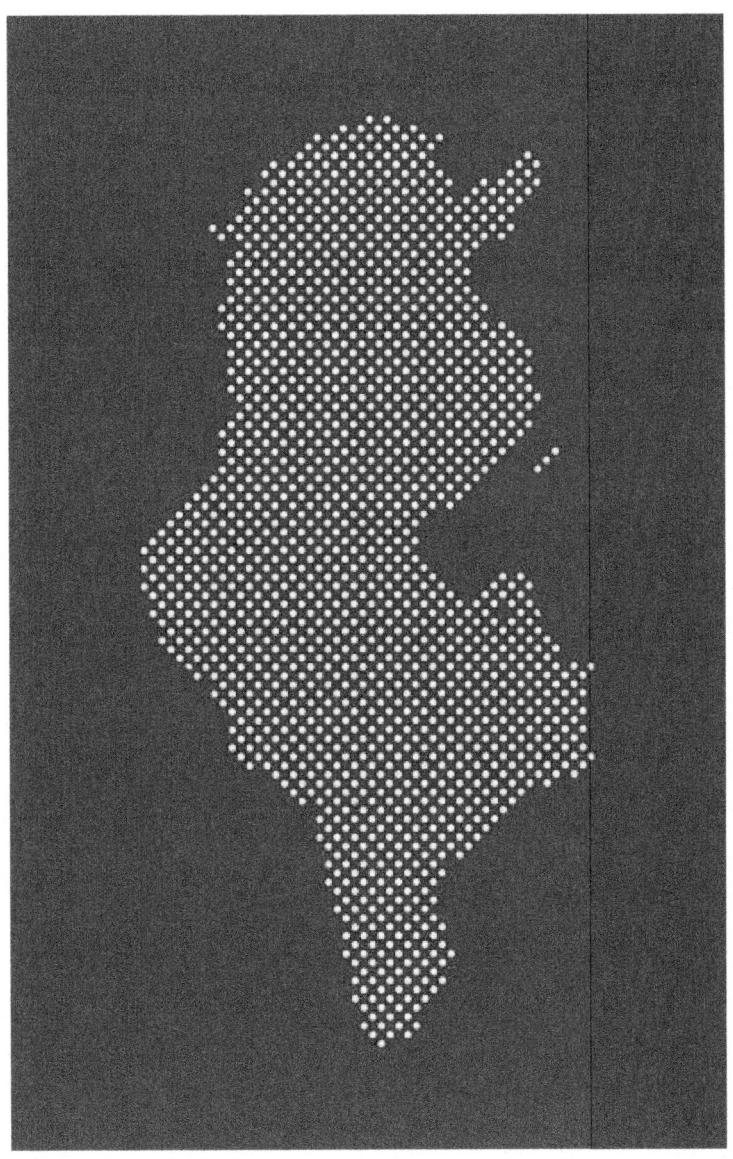

Travel planning websites and forums such as TripAdvisor, Lonely Planet's Thorn Tree, and regional platforms specific to Tunisia continue to be valuable sources of advice and up-to-date reviews. In 2026, social media platforms like Instagram and TikTok also serve as informal travel tools, giving visitors real-time glimpses into current festivals, food trends, or hidden spots around the city. Together, these apps and online tools form a digital safety net, ensuring travelers never feel lost or disconnected in Tunis.

10.2 Embassies and Consulates in Tunis

For international travelers, embassies and consulates serve as crucial lifelines in case of emergencies, legal issues, or even the loss of important documents like passports. Tunis, being the capital, hosts a wide range of foreign diplomatic missions. Most European, African, and Middle Eastern nations have embassies in the city, as well as consulates representing countries from Asia and the Americas. These institutions not only provide emergency support but also act as a source of valuable information on safety, local regulations, and travel advisories.

It is highly advisable for travelers to make note of the location, contact numbers, and opening hours of their respective embassies before arriving. In many cases, embassies can assist with passport renewals, emergency travel documents, medical assistance, and advice in situations of civil unrest or natural disasters. Many embassies in Tunis also provide newsletters or digital platforms where travelers can register their presence, ensuring they receive real-time updates or alerts during their stay. Having this resource in hand adds a layer of security and peace of mind, particularly for first-time visitors to Tunisia.

10.3 Tourist Information Centers

Tourist information centers in Tunis are scattered across key areas such as the Medina, Avenue Habib Bourguiba, and Tunis-Carthage International Airport. These centers are invaluable hubs for travelers seeking both practical assistance and insider tips. Staffed by professionals fluent in several languages, they provide maps, brochures, event calendars, and advice on local tours. They also help travelers book guided experiences, from cultural walks in the Medina to day trips to Dougga or Hammamet.

In addition to physical offices, Tunisia's Ministry of Tourism operates a robust online presence, offering digital brochures, interactive maps, and updates about events happening throughout the year. Many centers are now equipped with self-service kiosks that allow travelers to print directions, buy metro passes, or download information to their smartphones. For visitors who prefer personal interaction, staff members often go beyond basic assistance, sharing personal recommendations for restaurants, cafés, or lesser-known attractions that might not appear in guidebooks.

These centers are particularly helpful for last-minute changes in plans. For instance, if weather conditions cancel a boat trip, the staff can suggest alternative cultural activities or recommend seasonal events taking place in the city. For many travelers, stopping by a tourist information center early in their trip sets the tone for a more organized and rewarding experience in Tunis.

10.4 Packing Lists and Trip Planning for Tunis 2026

Packing for Tunis requires careful consideration of the city's Mediterranean climate, cultural norms, and the wide variety of activities a traveler might undertake. Light clothing is suitable for the hot summer months, but modest attire is recommended when visiting religious sites, the Medina, or rural areas. For women, scarves can be particularly useful both as a sign of respect in certain spaces and as practical protection against the sun. During spring and autumn, layers are essential, as the weather can shift from warm afternoons to cooler evenings. Winters are generally mild but can be damp, so a light jacket or raincoat is advisable.

Essential items include comfortable walking shoes, especially for navigating the cobblestone alleys of the old city and the ruins of Carthage. Sun protection is vital: hats, sunglasses, and sunscreen will ensure a more pleasant experience during outdoor explorations. Since Tunis offers both urban experiences and nearby seaside escapes, packing swimwear and beach essentials is a good idea. In 2026, with increasing eco-consciousness, reusable water bottles, shopping bags, and portable cutlery sets are recommended for those wishing to minimize their environmental impact while traveling.

Travel adapters are a necessity, as Tunisia uses European-style two-pin plugs. A portable charger or power bank is another useful addition, given how often travelers rely on their smartphones for navigation, translations, and photography. For those who wish to capture the vibrant colors of Tunis beyond their phones, a camera with a wide lens can do justice to the expansive landscapes of the Gulf of Tunis and the narrow, colorful lanes of Sidi Bou Said.

When planning a trip, travelers should consider creating a flexible itinerary that balances sightseeing with relaxation. While it is tempting to rush from one monument to another, Tunis rewards those who take time to linger in a café, watch the local rhythms of daily life, or strike up conversations with residents. A good travel plan also factors in day trips, as destinations like Carthage, La Marsa, and Dougga are within easy reach of the capital.

Finally, comprehensive travel insurance remains a crucial element of preparation, covering everything from medical emergencies to theft or cancellation. Having digital and physical copies of travel documents, booking confirmations, and insurance details ensures peace of mind throughout the journey. By thoughtfully packing and planning, visitors to Tunis in 2026 can focus on discovery, adventure, and cultural immersion, confident that they are well-prepared for whatever experiences await.

Printed in Dunstable, United Kingdom

76425538R00057